John G. Lake:
Powerful Faith-Building Quotes
From One of the Leading Classic
Charismatic Ministers
of All Time

Harrison House
Tulsa, Oklahoma

3rd Printing
Over 30,000 in Print

John G. Lake: Powerful Faith-Building Quotes
From One of the Leading Classic Charismatic Ministers of All Time
ISBN 0-89274-985-7
Copyright © 1996 by **Harrison House, Inc.**
P. O. Box 35035
Tulsa, Oklahoma 74153

Introduction

This book is a power-packed collection of faith-building quotes, stories, and short teachings taken from the life and ministry of John G. Lake. These teachings, stories, and quotes coupled with Scriptures will give you divine insight into one of the greatest miracle-healing ministries of the early 1900s in America.

This little book will encourage you and energize your faith to expect the same spirit of boldness and dominion that operated in John G. Lake's life and ministry to operate in yours. These short insights will help move you into action to believe God for the impossible in your life and see manifestations of the Spirit similar to the ones that took place in John G. Lake's life.

John G. Lake

John G. Lake was born in 1870 in Ontario, Canada, and moved to the United States with his family in 1886. In 1893 he married and became a successful businessman at his young age. As a result of several remarkable healings of family members, including his wife, under the ministry of John Alexander Dowie, he quit his successful business career and went into full-time ministry.

As a young man, Lake was always hungry for the things of God. That hunger led him to be baptized in the Holy Spirit in 1907. A year later, Lake took his family to South Africa to begin a missionary work. In just a few years he established a flourishing work which included the pioneering of more than 625 churches under his leadership. After returning from an expedition to the Kalahari Desert, he received the sad news that while he had been gone, his wife had died unexpectedly from a stroke and been buried.

Lake moved back to the United States and later remarried in 1913, settling in Spokane, Washington, where he established a healing ministry. More than 100,000 healings were recorded there during a five-year period of time. Later he founded works in Portland, Oregon, and San Diego, California, but returned to Spokane in 1931 where he died in 1935.

John G. Lake's life and ministry stand as an example for all Christians of the extent of God's power available to those who highly regard, believe and act on His Word.

In the Church divine healing is not an end in itself but a means to an end — Health.

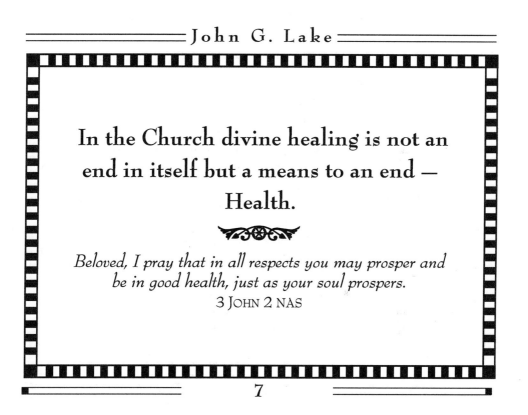

Beloved, I pray that in all respects you may prosper and be in good health, just as your soul prospers.
3 John 2 NAS

Oh, if I had one gift, or one desire that I would bestow on you, more than all others, I would bestow upon you the hunger for God.

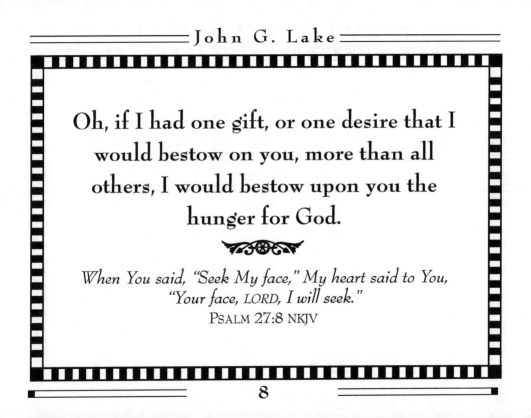

When You said, "Seek My face," My heart said to You, "Your face, LORD, I will seek."
PSALM 27:8 NKJV

Men are afraid of God because of wrong concepts. Let a man meet God in Jesus and he will love God.

Jesus said to him, "Have I been so long with you, and yet you have not come to know Me, Philip? He who has seen Me has seen the Father; how do you say, 'Show us the Father'?"

JOHN 14:9 NAS

The Father's heart did not need any moving toward the heart of man, for Jesus Christ, instead of moving the heart of the Father, was the MOVEMENT of God in behalf of mankind.

For God so loved the world, that he gave his only begotten Son, that whosoever believeth in him should not perish, but have everlasting life.
JOHN 3:16

You have just as much right to step into . . . God Almighty's presence as Jesus has . . . . Satan cannot stand before you any more than he can stand before Jesus.

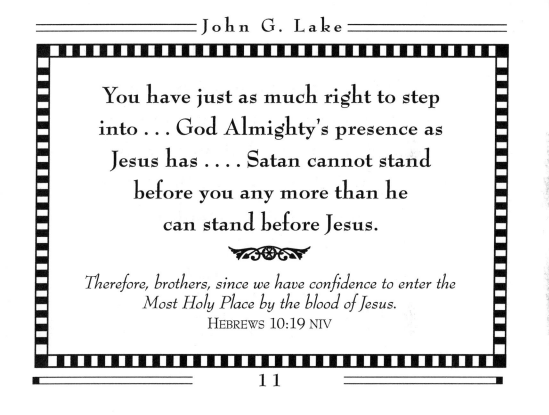

Therefore, brothers, since we have confidence to enter the Most Holy Place by the blood of Jesus.
HEBREWS 10:19 NIV

You can manufacture all the ordinances on earth, all the symbols there ever were until you become dazed and you lose yourself in the maze of them, and still you must find God.

For whoso findeth me findeth life, and shall obtain favour of the LORD.
PROVERBS 8:35

The test of the Spirit, and the only test of the Spirit Jesus ever gave, is the ultimate and final test. He said. "Ye shall know them by their fruits. Do men gather grapes of thorns, or figs of thistles?"

Ye shall know them by their fruits . . . . Even so every good tree bringeth forth good fruit; but a corrupt tree bringeth forth evil fruit. A good tree cannot bring forth evil fruit, neither can a corrupt tree bring forth good fruit . . . . Wherefore by their fruits ye shall know them.
MATTHEW 7:16-18,20

Men's writings grow old and out of date.
God's truth is ever fresh.

*The grass withereth, the flower fadeth:
but the word of our God shall stand for ever.*
ISAIAH 40:8

The tangibility of the Spirit of God is the scientific secret of healing.

And God wrought special miracles by the hands of Paul: So that from his body were brought unto the sick handkerchiefs or aprons, and the diseases departed from them, and the evil spirits went out of them.
ACTS 19:11,12

Distance is no barrier to God. Distance makes no difference. The Spirit of God in you will go as far as your love reaches.

The centurion answered and said, Lord, I am not worthy that thou shouldest come under my roof: but speak the word only, and my servant shall be healed.
MATTHEW 8:8

It is the Spirit of God that inhabits
the words, that speaks to the spirit
of another and reveals Christ
in and through him.

*And my speech and my preaching was not
with enticing words of man's wisdom, but
in demonstration of the Spirit and of power.*
1 CORINTHIANS 2:4

If there were any foundation whatever for the foolish belief that only Jesus and the apostles healed, the appointment of these seventy should settle it.

The seventy returned with joy, saying, "Lord, in your name even the demons submit to us!"
LUKE 10:17 NRSV

God's purpose in the creation of mankind was to develop an association on His own plane. Otherwise God would have been eternally living with babies or imbeciles.

And God said, Let us make man in our image, after our likeness: and let them have dominion over the fish of the sea, and over the fowl of the air, and over the cattle, and over all the earth, and over every creeping thing that creepeth upon the earth.
GENESIS 1:26

The spiritual action that takes place within the nature of man, that strong desire for God . . . causes everything else, perhaps unconsciously to himself, to become secondary.

Blessed are they which do hunger and thirst after righteousness: for they shall be filled.
MATTHEW 5:6

Other souls may shatter on the rocks; other souls may wither in disappointment, but the lives that have been planted in that spirit of divine fidelity to Jesus Christ are unconquerable.

For he shall be as a tree planted by the waters, and that spreadeth out her roots by the river, and shall not see when heat cometh, but her leaf shall be green; and shall not be careful in the year of drought, neither shall cease from yielding fruit.
JEREMIAH 17:8

Healing in any department of the nature, whether spirit, soul or body, is but a means to an end. The object of healing is health, abiding health of body, soul and spirit. The healing of the spirit unites the spirit of man to God forever. The healing of the soul corrects psychic disorder and brings the soul processes into harmony with the mind of God. And the healing of the body completes the union of man with God when the Holy Spirit possesses all.

I want to tell you, when you begin to analyze the subject of sickness, you will discover that usually the difficulty is that there is sin behind it. Not necessarily that there is an act of sin or some personal sin, but more likely the laziness of our soul, or the inactivity of our spirit, or neglect of God's Word, or neglect of faith and love and prayer. These are the things that usually underlie and generate difficulties in men's lives.

Christianity is one hundred percent supernatural — God possessing man.

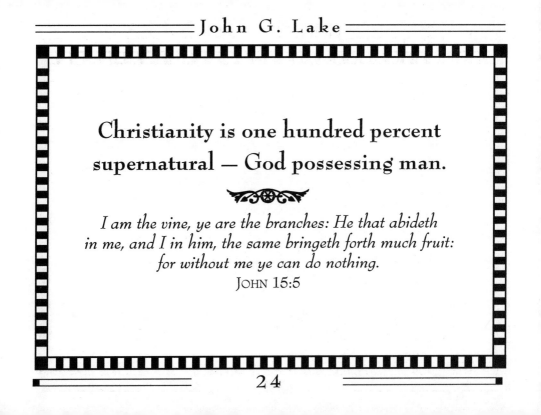

I am the vine, ye are the branches: He that abideth in me, and I in him, the same bringeth forth much fruit: for without me ye can do nothing.

JOHN 15:5

Jesus Christ is at once the law and life of God.

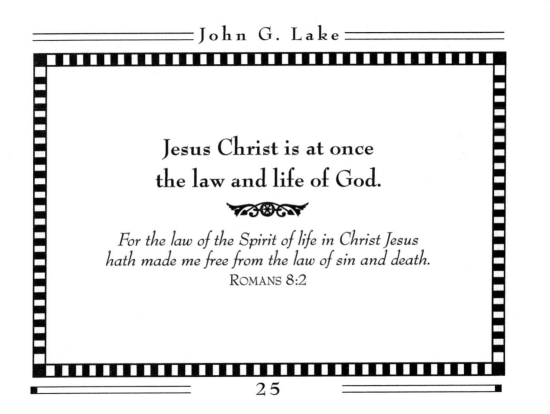

For the law of the Spirit of life in Christ Jesus hath made me free from the law of sin and death.
ROMANS 8:2

You do not have to pump faith into a man when his sin is taken away and his disobedience is gone, bless God.

But, dearly loved friends, if our consciences are clear, we can come to the Lord with perfect assurance and trust.
1 JOHN 3:21 TLB

Obedience to the Word of God is the first principle upon which relationship with God is established.

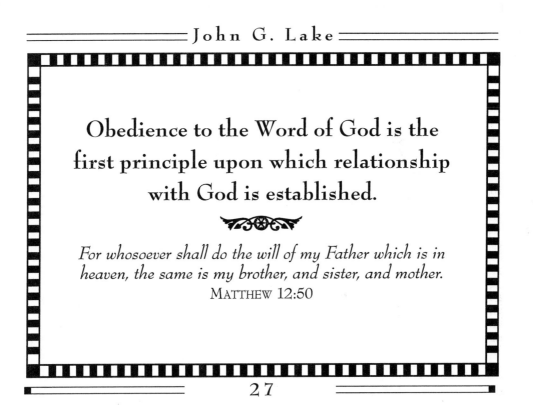

For whosoever shall do the will of my Father which is in heaven, the same is my brother, and sister, and mother.
MATTHEW 12:50

Everything that Jesus did was the will and the word of the Father. So everything the Christian does, if he is a real one, should be the will and word of Jesus Christ.

For I have left Heaven and have come down to earth not to seek my own pleasure, but to do the will of Him who sent me.
JOHN 6:38 WEYMOUTH

Observation demonstrates that the really great in God who bless mankind are those who live in absolute accordance with the teachings of Jesus.

Whosoever therefore shall break one of these least commandments, and shall teach men so, he shall be called the least in the kingdom of heaven: but whosoever shall do and teach them, the same shall be called great in the kingdom of heaven.
MATTHEW 5:19

If for five minutes God's spiritual
illumination could come over our souls,
and our consciousness be awakened . . .
there isn't a man or woman in this
house that would not fall prostrate
on their face before God.

And the light shineth in darkness;
and the darkness comprehended it not.
JOHN 1:5

People talk about the heaven they are going to, but I want to tell you that heaven is right here when the consciousness is awakened to comprehend and understand and realize what our environment in the Spirit is.

Thy kingdom come. Thy will be done,
On earth as it is in heaven.
MATTHEW 6:10 NAS

Varied philosophies have been
presented by various minds,
but the Christ imparted LIFE.

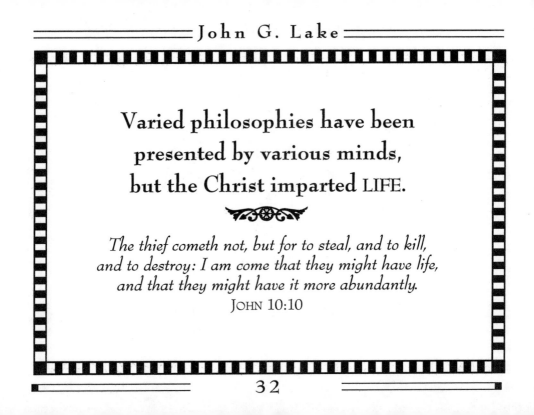

*The thief cometh not, but for to steal, and to kill,
and to destroy: I am come that they might have life,
and that they might have it more abundantly.*
JOHN 10:10

The Holy Ghost in the Christian
was to be as powerful as the
Holy Ghost was in the Christ.

*Verily, verily, I say unto you, He that believeth on me,
the works that I do shall he do also; and greater works
than these shall he do; because I go unto my Father.*
JOHN 14:12

Jesus Christ operates through you.
He does not operate independently of
you . . . . Man and God become united.

*I can do all things through Christ
which strengtheneth me.*
PHILIPPIANS 4:13

The world is awakening to the marvelous truth that Christ is not only in heaven, but that Christ is in you.

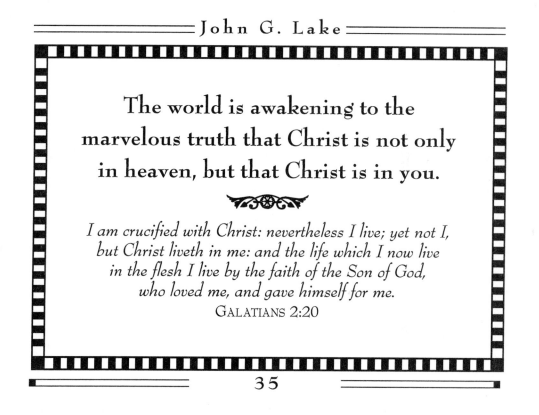

I am crucified with Christ: nevertheless I live; yet not I, but Christ liveth in me: and the life which I now live in the flesh I live by the faith of the Son of God, who loved me, and gave himself for me.
GALATIANS 2:20

According to the degree of faith in your
soul, so that action, or interaction,
of the Spirit of God in your life
for healing will be great or small.

*Then touched he their eyes, saying,
According to your faith be it unto you.
And their eyes were opened; and Jesus straitly
charged them, saying, See that no man know it.*
MATTHEW 9:29,30

When I saw for the first time by the Word of God that sickness was not the Will of God . . . everything in my nature rose up to defeat the will of the devil.

And Caleb stilled the people before Moses,
and said, Let us go up at once, and possess it;
for we are well able to overcome it.
NUMBERS 13:30

Whenever I reach a place where I lose my appetite for the Book, and rather talk with people than read the Bible, or rather read books about the Bible than to read the Bible, then I know I am backslidden in my spirit.

The backslider in heart shall be filled with his own ways: and a good man shall be satisfied from himself.
PROVERBS 14:14

The reason people become sick is the same reason that they become sinful. They surrender to the suggestion of the thing that is evil, and it takes possession of the heart.

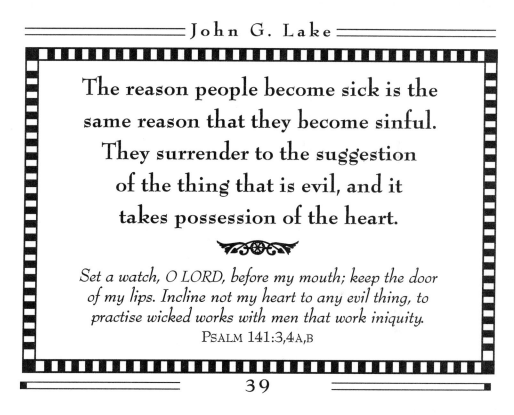

Set a watch, O LORD, before my mouth; keep the door of my lips. Incline not my heart to any evil thing, to practise wicked works with men that work iniquity.
PSALM 141:3,4A,B

A few months ago I was absent from the city of Spokane, and when I returned Mrs. Lake was not at home. It was just about time to leave for my afternoon service. Just then someone came in and said, "Your secretary, Mrs. Graham, is in the throes of death, and your wife is with her." So I hurried down to the place. When I got there the wife of one of my ministers met me at the door and said, "You are too late; she has gone." And as I stepped in I met the minister coming out of the room. He said, "She has not breathed for a long time." But as I looked on that woman, and thought how God Almighty three years before had raised that woman out of death, after her womb and ovaries and tubes had been removed in operations, and God Almighty had given them back to her, after which she married and conceived; how my heart flamed. I took that woman up off that pillow, and called on God for the lightnings of heaven to blast the power of death and deliver her, and I commanded her to come back and stay, and she came back after not breathing for 23 minutes.

There is a mighty lot of difference between saying prayers and praying.

And the prayer of faith shall save the sick, and the Lord shall raise him up; and if he have committed sins, they shall be forgiven him.
JAMES 5:15

God will answer the heart that cries;
God will answer the soul that asks.

*Evening and morning and at noon I will pray,
and cry aloud, And He shall hear my voice.*
PSALM 55:17 NKJV

God never intended that the outer man
of the flesh should be the governor of
the great man of the soul or spirit.

*For the mind set on the flesh is death, but the
mind set on the Spirit is life and peace.*
ROMANS 8:6 NAS

No man ever successfully governed
another life until he was first able
to govern himself.

*He that is slow to anger is better than the mighty; and he
that ruleth his spirit than he that taketh a city.*
PROVERBS 16:32

It is not TRY but TRUST .... It is not trying to get healed. It is trusting Him for it, and believing Him when He says He will do it ....

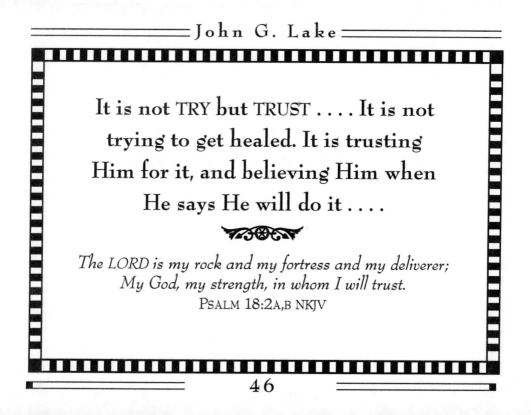

The LORD is my rock and my fortress and my deliverer; My God, my strength, in whom I will trust.
PSALM 18:2A,B NKJV

Now healing is not a difficult matter.
It does not take a bit more faith to be
healed from your sickness that it does
to be saved from your sins.

*For with their hearts men believe and so attain to
righteousness, while with their lips they make their
Profession of Faith and so find Salvation.*
ROMANS 10:10 TWENTIETH CENTURY

In those early centuries of Christianity, Christianity did not go into the world apologizing. It went to slay the powers of darkness and undo the works of the devil, and it lived in holy triumph.

And Jesus came and spake unto them, saying, All power is given unto me in heaven and in earth. Go ye therefore, and teach all nations, baptizing them in the name of the Father, and of the Son, and of the Holy Ghost.
MATTHEW 28:18,19

When you and I are lost in the Son of
God and the fires of Jesus burn in our
hearts, as they did in His, our words
will be the words of Spirit and of life.
There will be no death in them.

*And you show that you are a letter of Christ, prepared
by us, written not with ink but with the Spirit of the
living God, not on tablets of stone but on tablets of human
hearts . . . . who has made us competent to be ministers
of a new covenant, not of letter but of spirit;
for the letter kills, but the Spirit gives life.*

2 CORINTHIANS 3:3,6 NRSV

I feel that very frequently prayer is made a refuge to dodge the action of faith.

If you believe, you will receive whatever you ask for in prayer.
MATTHEW 21:22 NIV

"If" always doubts. The prayer
of faith has no "ifs" in it.

"Lord, if You are willing, You can make me clean."
And He stretched out His hand and touched him,
saying, "I am willing; be cleansed." And immediately
his leprosy was cleansed.
MATTHEW 8:2B,3 NAS

Instead of Christians taking the responsibility, they try to put the responsibility on God.

But without faith it is impossible to please him: for he that cometh to God must believe that he is, and that he is a rewarder of them that diligently seek him.
HEBREWS 11:6

Everything in the world of God
that ever was possible to the Lord
Jesus Christ is likewise possible
to the Christian.

*Most assuredly, I say to you, he who believes in Me, the
works that I do he will do also; and greater works than
these he will do, because I go to My Father.*
JOHN 14:12 NKJV

I not only believe in healing of disease but believe that through faith in God we can be rendered virtually immune from disease and contagion.

We know that anyone who is born of God does not sin; He who was born of God preserves him, and the evil One never catches him.
1 JOHN 5:18 MOFFATT

When we are in right communion and fellowship with the Lord, there is not power enough in all hell to put disease upon our little finger.

We know [absolutely] that anyone born of God does not [deliberately and knowingly] practice committing sin, but the One Who was begotten of God carefully watches over and protects him [Christ's divine presence within him preserves him against the evil], and the wicked one does not lay hold (get a grip) on him or touch [him].

1 JOHN 5:18 AMP

God thinks in accordance with the heavenly purity of His own nature. Man thinks in accordance with that degree of purity that his soul realizes. But the ultimate note is in God.

If then you have been raised up with Christ, keep seeking the things above, where Christ is, seated at the right hand of God. Set your mind on the things above, not on the things that are on earth.

COLOSSIANS 3:1,2 NAS

The development of the soul into the likeness and stature of Christ is then the greatest element and purpose that can enter our lives. God Himself puts it first; man ought not to put it second.

As newborn babes, desire the pure milk of the word, that you may grow thereby.
1 PETER 2:2 NKJV

If you have doubts, questions, and fears concerning the Bible and its inspiration, we know that if one soul ever heard from heaven, another soul may.
If one soul ever had an interview with God, another soul may.
If any man ever knew his sins were forgiven at any period, another man may know his sins are forgiven now.
If a man or woman ever was healed by the power of God, then men and women can be healed again.

Many look forward to the second coming of Jesus as though mechanically, on a certain date, when certain events come to pass, Jesus is going to appear. I do not see it that way. I believe there must be an overwhelming hunger for the Lord's coming in the hearts of men so that a prayer such as was never prayed in the world before for Christ to come will rise to heaven. And when it rises to heaven on the part of sufficient souls, it will take Jesus Christ off the throne and bring Him down to earth.

Your knowledge may give you ground for faith, but faith is resident in your spirit.

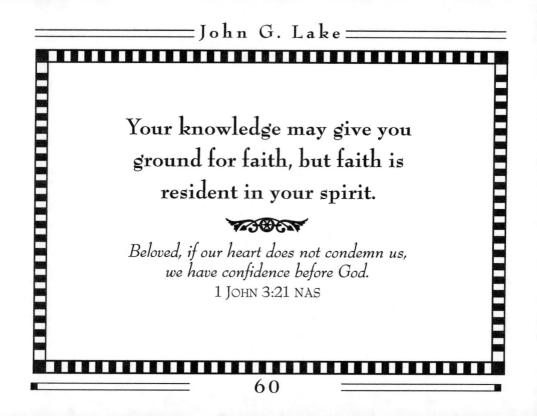

Beloved, if our heart does not condemn us, we have confidence before God.
1 JOHN 3:21 NAS

Beloved, faith is more important
than power. Faith commands
power and vitalizes it.

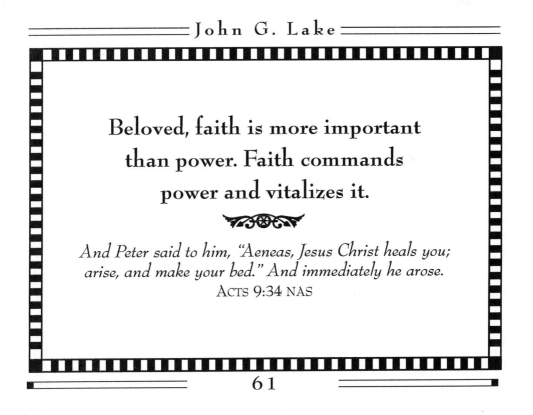

And Peter said to him, "Aeneas, Jesus Christ heals you;
arise, and make your bed." And immediately he arose.
ACTS 9:34 NAS

Corroding cares come and get in around your spirit life, and it just covers you and breaks your connection with the Lord.

And the cares of this world, the deceitfulness of riches, and the desires for other things entering in choke the word, and it becomes unfruitful.
MARK 4:19 NKJV

Fear of the oppressor is foolishness.
People are worried about things
that never come to pass. What a
waste of life to worry!

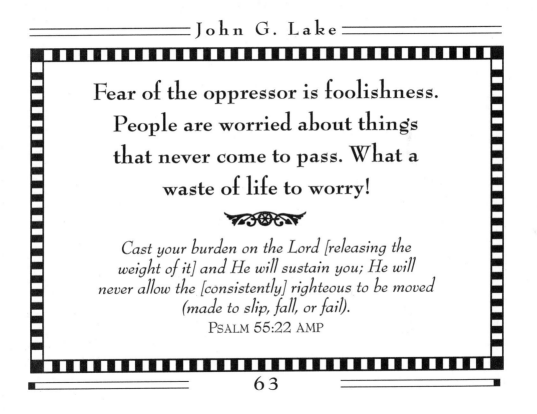

*Cast your burden on the Lord [releasing the
weight of it] and He will sustain you; He will
never allow the [consistently] righteous to be moved
(made to slip, fall, or fail).*
PSALM 55:22 AMP

There never has been a man
in the world who was converted,
and was sick at the same time,
who might not have been healed
if he had believed God for it.

Bless the LORD, O my soul, and forget not all his benefits: Who forgiveth all thine iniquities; who healeth all thy diseases.
PSALM 103:2,3

The Holy Spirit coming into the person of a sick one comes as a living, creative power. It is the Creation of life in them that drives out disease.

It is the Spirit Who gives life [He is the Life-giver]; the flesh conveys no benefit whatever [there is no profit in it]. The words (truths) that I have been speaking to you are spirit and life.
JOHN 6:63 AMP

Beloved, it is not our long prayers, but believing God that gets the answer.

Let us draw near to God with a sincere heart in full assurance of faith, having our hearts sprinkled to cleanse us from a guilty conscience and having our bodies washed with pure water.
HEBREWS 10:22 NIV

Those who teach that the day of miracles is past, teach the most disastrous lie that was ever told . . . . Such lies are responsible for the prevalent lack of faith in God and have robbed Christianity of the power to demonstrate itself.

Jesus Christ the same yesterday, and to day, and for ever.
HEBREWS 13:8

Healing is not always obtained
by saying a prayer. It is obtained
by obeying God.

My son, forget not my law; but let thine heart
keep my commandments: For length of days,
and long life, and peace, shall they add to thee.
PROVERBS 3:1,2

Miracles are creative. Healing is the
restoration of what has been.

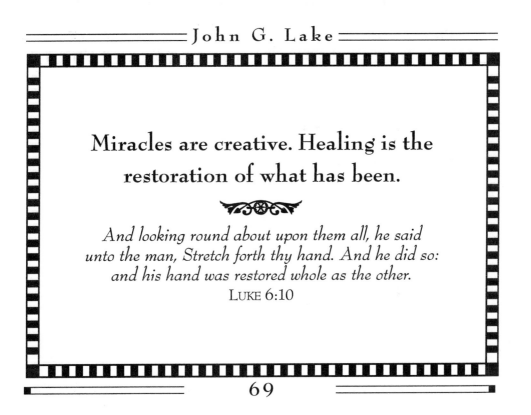

*And looking round about upon them all, he said
unto the man, Stretch forth thy hand. And he did so:
and his hand was restored whole as the other.*
LUKE 6:10

Jesus did not come with a club, but with the great loving heart of the Son of God. He was "moved with compassion."

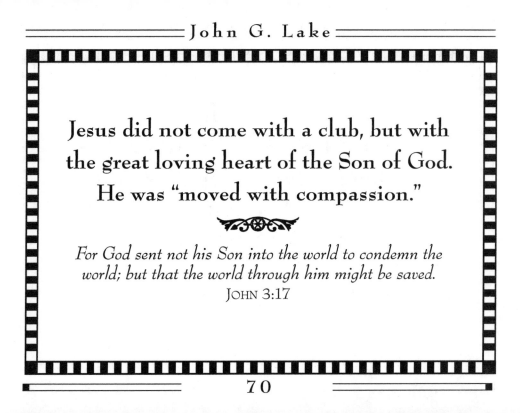

For God sent not his Son into the world to condemn the world; but that the world through him might be saved.
JOHN 3:17

There is no substitute for the love of God. You have the capacity to love. All the action of the Spirit of God has its secret there.

Such a hope is no mockery, because God's love has flooded our inmost heart through the Holy Spirit he has given us.
ROMANS 5:5 NEB

The nearer the soul is to God, the less its perturbations; as the point nearest the center of a circle is subject to the least motion.

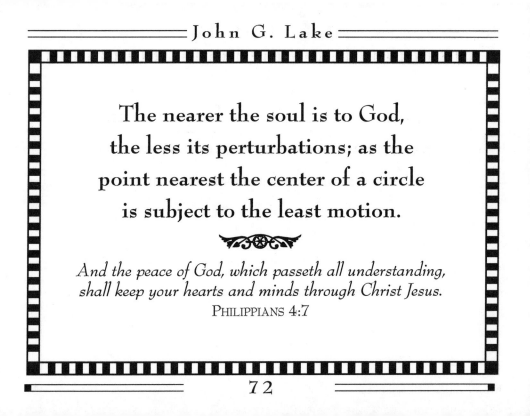

And the peace of God, which passeth all understanding, shall keep your hearts and minds through Christ Jesus.
PHILIPPIANS 4:7

Compassion reaches further than law, further than demands of judges. Compassion reaches to the heart of life, to the secret of our being.

But a certain Samaritan, as he journeyed, came where he was: and when he saw him, he had compassion on him.
LUKE 10:33

Men, by the action of the will, take themselves out of the control of the power of the law of sin and death, and by the action of their will place themselves consciously in union and in touch with the law of the Spirit of Life.

For the new spiritual principle of life "in" Christ Jesus lifts me out of the old vicious circle of sin and death.

ROMANS 8:2 PHILLIPS

The man with Christ in him, the Holy Ghost, is greater than any other power in the world. All other natural and evil powers are less than God; even Satan himself is a lesser power. Man with God in him is greater than Satan.

Ye are of God, little children, and have overcome them: because greater is he that is in you, than he that is in the world.

1 JOHN 4:4

Now comes one of the most remarkable cases in history. The Risdon family stand holding their six-year-old son on their shoulders. This boy was born with a closed head. In consequence, as he increased in years, the skull was forced upward like the roof of a house, the forehead and the back of the head also being forced out in similar manner, giving the head the appearance of the hull of a yacht upside down. The pressure on the brain caused the right side to become paralyzed and the child was dumb. Physicians said that nothing could be done for him until he was 12 years old, and then the entire top of the head would have to be removed, the sides of the skull expanded, and the entire head covered with a silver plate. Under Divine Healing ministration in answer to prayer the bones softened, the head expanded, the skull was reduced to its normal size, the paralysis disappeared, the dumbness was gone. He spoke like other children and afterwards attended the public school.

You must take Christ as your Healer —

not as an experiment.

But when Jesus heard it, he answered him, saying,
Fear not: believe only, and she shall be made whole.
LUKE 8:50

I regard the healing of a man's
body to be just as sacred as
the healing of his soul.

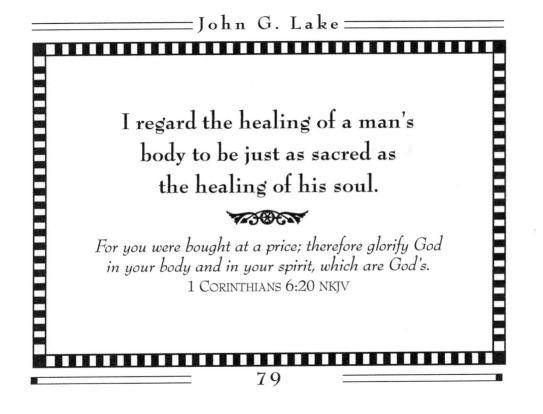

*For you were bought at a price; therefore glorify God
in your body and in your spirit, which are God's.*
1 CORINTHIANS 6:20 NKJV

It is not the words you say that are going to bless them. They are in need of something greater — love.

Let us, then, go to him outside the camp, bearing the disgrace he bore.
HEBREWS 13:13 NIV

Mankind has one supreme need,
and that is the love of God.
The hearts of men are dying
for lack of the love of God.

But God demonstrates His own love toward us, in that while we were yet sinners, Christ died for us.
ROMANS 5:8 NAS

Jesus Christ never wasted His time establishing mere morality. Jesus Christ, the Son of God, declared IMMORTALITY to be the goal of Christianity . . . .

And I give unto them eternal life; and they shall never perish, neither shall any man pluck them out of my hand.
JOHN 10:28

Your soul will never demonstrate the power of God in any appreciable degree until it conceives and understands the real vision of Christ.

But I certify you, brethren, that the gospel which was preached of me is not after man. For I neither received it of man, neither was I taught it, but by the revelation of Jesus Christ.
GALATIANS 1:11,12

The value of the ministry of healing is not in the mere fact that people are healed. The value of healing is more largely in the fact that it becomes a demonstration of the living, inner, vital power of God, which should dwell in every life and make us new and mighty men in the hands of God.

Then Jesus answering said unto them,
Go your way, and tell John what things ye have
seen and heard; how that the blind see, the lame walk,
the lepers are cleansed, the deaf hear, the dead
are raised, to the poor the gospel is preached.
LUKE 7:22

A closing sentence of an interpretation of tongues given in June, 1910, in Somerset, East Cape Colony, South Africa: "Christ is at once the spotless descent of God into man, and the sinless ascent of man into God, and the Holy Spirit is the Agent by whom this is accomplished."

And he that keepeth his commandments dwelleth in him, and he in him. And hereby we know that he abideth in us, by the Spirit which he hath given us.
1 JOHN 3:24

The Christian with a groan in him
never moved the world except to groans.

Do all things without grumbling or questioning.
PHILIPPIANS 2:14A RSV

If there are any failures,
it is our failure, not God's.

*And those who know Your name will put their
trust in You; For You, LORD, have not forsaken
those who seek You.*
PSALM 9:10 NKJV

If there is something that is keeping you from being blessed, let clear go and let your hands and heart open.

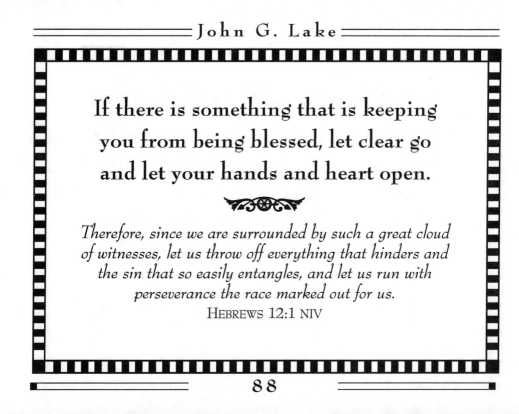

Therefore, since we are surrounded by such a great cloud of witnesses, let us throw off everything that hinders and the sin that so easily entangles, and let us run with perseverance the race marked out for us.
HEBREWS 12:1 NIV

A great many people lose the blessing that they might have had, by sticking their nose into other people's affairs.

And Miriam and Aaron spake against Moses because of the Ethiopian woman whom he had married: for he had married an Ethiopian woman. And they said, Hath the LORD indeed spoken only by Moses? hath he not spoken also by us? And the LORD heard it.

NUMBERS 12:1,2

Fear causes the spirit of man to lose its sense of dominion. It causes the mind of man to become subjective. It causes the person of man to become subservient.

And he said, I heard thy voice in the garden, and I was afraid, because I was naked; and I hid myself.
GENESIS 3:10

That which is in the inner life will also be revealed in the outer life. That which is a fact in the mental and psychological will become a fact in the physical also.

The good man brings good things out of the good stored up in his heart, and the evil man brings evil things out of the evil stored up in his heart. For out of the overflow of his heart his mouth speaks.

LUKE 6:45 NIV

I can see . . . that there is coming from heaven a new manifestation of the Holy Spirit in power, and that new manifestations will be in sweetness, in love, in tenderness . . . beyond anything your heart or mine ever saw. The very lightning of God will flash through men's souls.

And it shall come to pass afterward, that I will pour out my spirit upon all flesh; and your sons and your daughters shall prophesy, your old men shall dream dreams, your young men shall see visions.

JOEL 2:28

Now the Spirit of God radiates from the Christian's person because of the indwelling Holy Ghost, and makes him impregnable to any touch or contact of evil forces. He is the subjective force himself, the Spirit of God radiates from him as long as his faith in God is active.

For whatsoever is born of God overcometh the world . . . even our faith. Who is he that overcometh the world, but he that believeth that Jesus is the Son of God?
1 JOHN 5:4,5

Musicians talk of an ultimate note. It is a note not found on any keyboard. It is a peculiar note. A man sits down to tune a piano. He has no guide to the proper key; yet he has an inner guide. That guide is the note that he has in his soul. And the nearer he can bring his instrument into harmony with the note in his soul, the nearer he has attained perfection.

There is an ultimate note in the heart of the Christian. It is the note of conscious victory through Jesus Christ. The nearer our life is tuned to that note of conscious victory, the greater the victory that will be evidenced in our life.

Nearby a city in South Africa in which I was ministering were hills with out-croppings of rocks — like a series of cliffs, one above the other. I used to go up these to be alone and get some rest. One day I observed a lady bring a young child and set him on one of the shelves above a small cliff. She left him some water and food. It seemed a dangerous thing to do as the child might fall and hurt himself. However, I observed that the child was crippled and could not move around. I went over and laid my hands on the child and prayed. Immediately he bounded off down the hill to catch his mother. Not caring to meet anyone I moved around the hill out of sight.

God pulls you out of the river of sin and then must get the river out of you.

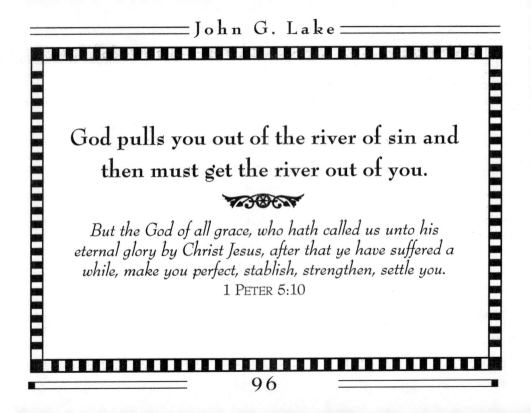

But the God of all grace, who hath called us unto his eternal glory by Christ Jesus, after that ye have suffered a while, make you perfect, stablish, strengthen, settle you.
1 PETER 5:10

Putting off the old man is
not a growth, it is a death.

*So you also must consider yourselves
dead to sin and alive to God in Christ Jesus.*
ROMANS 6:11 NRSV

The lightnings of Jesus heal men by its touch; sin dissolves, disease flees when the power of God approaches.

And the people all tried to touch him, because power was coming from him and healing them all.
LUKE 6:19 NIV

The minister of God who is afraid
to walk out and believe his God
and trust his God for results
is no Christian at all.

*Jesus said unto him, If thou canst believe,
all things are possible to him that believeth.*
MARK 9:23

When a Christian tries to live by
REASON he is moving out of God's
country into the enemy's land.
We belong in the miraculous or
supernatural realm.

For we guide our lives by faith, and not by what we see.
2 CORINTHIANS 5:7 TWENTIETH CENTURY

A weak Christianity always wants to drop to the imperfect, and adjust itself to the popular mind. But a real Christianity ever seeks to be made perfect in God.

Since we have these promises, dear friends, let us purify ourselves from everything that contaminates body and spirit, perfecting holiness out of reverence for God.
2 CORINTHIANS 7:1 NIV

The usual custom in the Modern Church is that when a preacher breaks out in a living faith and begins to get extraordinary answers to prayer, he is cautioned by the worldy wise, and if persistent, is eventually made to feel that he is regarded as strange. If he still persists, he is ostracized and actually dismissed by some churches and conferences.

Be not afraid of their faces: for I am with thee to deliver thee, saith the LORD.
JEREMIAH 1:8

Jesus Christ did not leave us in doubt about God's will, but when the Church lost her faith in God, she began to teach the people that maybe it was not God's will to heal them. So the Church introduced the phrase, "If it be Thy will" concerning healing. But Jesus healed all that came to Him. (Matthew 4:23; Luke 9:6,11).

Having a form of godliness, but denying the power thereof: from such turn away.
2 TIMOTHY 3:5

The more a Christian possesses,
the more of a servant he will be.

*For though I be free from all men, yet have I made
myself servant unto all, that I might gain the more.*
1 CORINTHIANS 9:19

The greatest and strongest and noblest
is always the humblest.

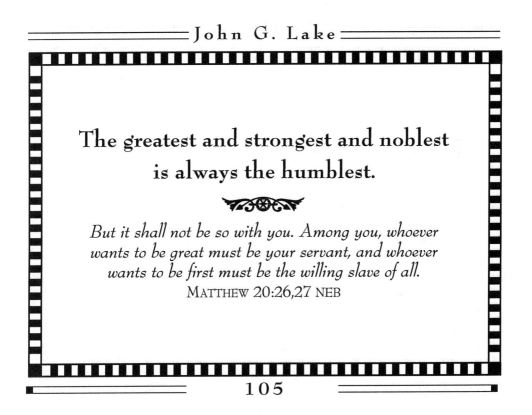

*But it shall not be so with you. Among you, whoever
wants to be great must be your servant, and whoever
wants to be first must be the willing slave of all.*
MATTHEW 20:26,27 NEB

If I could bring to you today one blessing greater than another, it would be the consciousness of trust in God.

Have not I commanded thee? Be strong and of a good courage; be not afraid, neither be thou dismayed: for the LORD thy God is with thee whithersoever thou goest.
JOSHUA 1:9

Faith is not manifested in shouts and yells . . . . It is the set faith of the soul that lays hold of God.

Only it must be in faith that he asks with no wavering (no hesitating, no doubting). For the one who wavers (hesitates, doubts) is like the billowing surge out at sea that is blown hither and thither and tossed by the wind.
JAMES 1:6 AMP

The reason that people do not have a rich, beautiful faith is that their spirit is denied the privilege of communion and fellowship with the Father.

He that dwelleth in the secret place of the most High shall abide under the shadow of the Almighty. I will say of the LORD, He is my refuge and my fortress: my God; in him will I trust.
PSALM 91:1,2

The most supreme example that God ever performed was His taking possession of men. By the Holy Spirit He comes in and takes possession of those who are hungry.

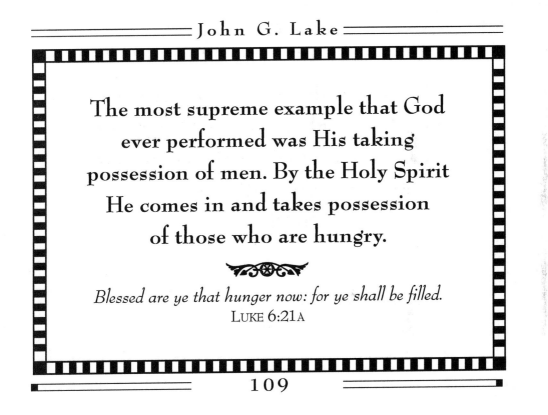

Blessed are ye that hunger now: for ye shall be filled.
LUKE 6:21A

This Word of God does not even give me the privilege of seeking guidance of angels, let alone the spirit of the dead, or the spirit of a living man either. It gives me one privilege. There is One Mind that knows all, that is the mind of God, and if I am His child, and if my heart is made pure by the blood of His Son, then I have a right to come into His presence and secure anything my heart may want.

And when they shall say unto you, Seek unto them that have familiar spirits, and unto wizards that peep, and that mutter: should not a people seek unto their God? for the living to the dead?

ISAIAH 8:19

Peter in his exposition of this fact, says, "By whose stripes ye were healed." The use of "were" in this text indicates that the healing was accomplished in the mind of God when Jesus Christ gave Himself as the eternal Sacrifice, and has never had to get done over again for the healing of any individual. He willed it once; it is done forever. It is yours to have, yours to enjoy, and yours to impart to others.

Who his own self bare our sins in his own body on the tree, that we, being dead to sins, should live unto righteousness: by whose stripes ye were healed.
1 PETER 2:24

During that great plague . . . they sent a government ship with supplies and a corps of doctors. One of the doctors sent for me, and said, "What have you been using to protect yourself? Our corps has this preventative and that, which we use as protection, but we concluded that if a man could stay on the ground as you have and keep ministering to the sick and burying the dead, you must have a secret. What is it?" I answered, "Brother, that is the 'law of the Spirit of life in Christ Jesus.' I believe that just as long as I keep my soul in contact with the living God so that His Spirit is flowing into my soul and body, that no germ will ever attach itself to me, for the Spirit of God will kill it."

He asked, "Don't you think that you had better use our preventatives?"

I replied, "No, but doctor I think that you would like to experiment with me. If you will go over to one of these dead people and take the foam that comes out of their lungs after death, then put it under the microscope you will see masses of living germs. You will find they are alive until a reasonable time after a man is dead. You can fill my hand with them and I will keep it under the microscope, and instead of these germs remaining alive, they will die instantly."

They tried it and found it was true. They questioned, "What is that?"

I replied, "That is 'the law of the Spirit of life in Christ Jesus.'" When a man's spirit and a man's body are filled with the blessed presence of God, it oozes out of the pores of your flesh and kills the germs."

Power manifests in many ways. There is the power of FAITH which draws to you what seems to be impossible.

And Jesus said unto them, Because of your unbelief: for verily I say unto you, If ye have faith as a grain of mustard seed, ye shall say unto this mountain, Remove hence to yonder place; and it shall remove; and nothing shall be impossible unto you.
MATTHEW 17:20

God is not confined to methods. Heaven bows to the soul with faith anywhere, under any circumstances.

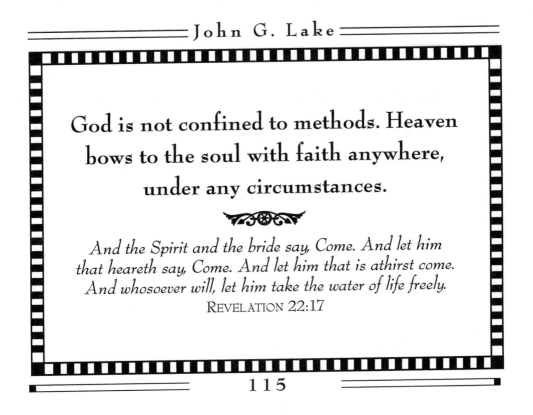

And the Spirit and the bride say, Come. And let him that heareth say, Come. And let him that is athirst come. And whosoever will, let him take the water of life freely.
REVELATION 22:17

Fear of the devil is nonsense. Fear of demons is foolish. The Spirit of God anointing the Christian heart makes the soul impregnable to the powers of darkness.

No weapon that is formed against thee shall prosper; and every tongue that shall rise against thee in judgment thou shalt condemn.
ISAIAH 54:17A

Most of our difficulties are the difficulties that we anticipate or fear are coming tomorrow .... Do not worry about tomorrow. Rest down in God.

Therefore do not worry about tomorrow, for tomorrow will worry about itself. Each day has enough trouble of its own.
MATTHEW 6:34 NIV

When faith and Spirit come together, there is an interaction . . . a movement of God . . . a manifestation of the Spirit . . . a divine explosion! FAITH AND GOD UNITED IS DIVINE HEALING.

For we also have had the gospel preached to us, just as they did; but the message they heard was of no value to them, because those who heard did not combine it with faith.

HEBREWS 4:2 NIV

Jesus did not heal the sick in order to coax them to be Christians. He healed because it was His nature to heal. The multitude surrounded Him. His love gushed forth like an electric billow.

And the whole multitude sought to touch him: for there went virtue out of him, and healed them all.
LUKE 6:19

It doesn't make any difference how sick
you are, there is healing for you if you
are in contact with the Healer.

*But Jesus told him, "No, it was someone who deliberately
touched me, for I felt healing power go out from me."*
LUKE 8:46 TLB

Sickness is the result of sin.
There could have been no sickness
if there had been no sin.

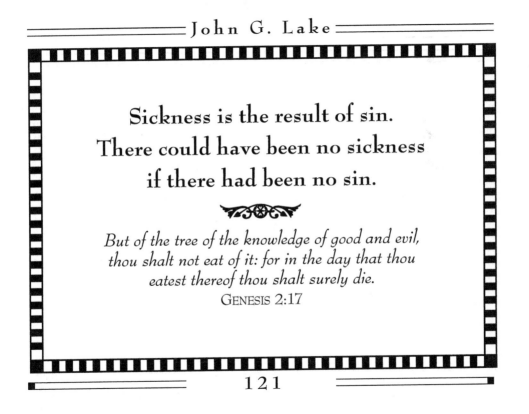

*But of the tree of the knowledge of good and evil,
thou shalt not eat of it: for in the day that thou
eatest thereof thou shalt surely die.*
GENESIS 2:17

When there is any other spirit that comes into the church, it is not the spirit of Christianity. It is a foreign spirit. It is a sissified substitute.

Beloved, believe not every spirit, but try the spirits whether they are of God: because many false prophets are gone out into the world.
1 JOHN 4:1

It is not necessary for people to be dominated by evil, nor by evil spirits. Instead of being dominated, Christians should exercise dominion and control other forces.

He called the twelve and began to send them out two by two, and gave them authority over the unclean spirits.
MARK 6:7 NRSV

Someone asks: "What does it mean to cast out devils?" It means that the man with the Holy Ghost dwelling in him is the master, and has dominion over every devilish force and counterfeit.

Calling his twelve Disciples to him, Jesus gave them authority over foul spirits, so that they could drive them out, as well as the power of curing every kind of disease and every kind of sickness.

MATTHEW 10:1 TWENTIETH CENTURY

I do not spend much time in talking about the devil. The Lord took care of him. He [Jesus] has the keys of hell and death, and He has mastered that individual and that condition once and for all.

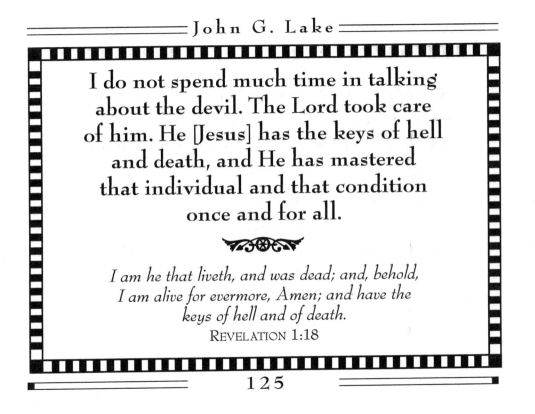

I am he that liveth, and was dead; and, behold, I am alive for evermore, Amen; and have the keys of hell and of death.
REVELATION 1:18

Now if your spirit has reached the place where it has no appetite for the things of God, you have been playing hooky. You have been feeding on things that you ought not to eat, and you have compelled your poor spirit to feed on trash, cheap scandal, useless talk, and wisecracking. You have never given your spirit any real, healthy food for a long time. The poor thing is dying of hunger. The doctor then told of an experience he had down in Texas where a whole congregation had come, practically all of them for healing. He told them,

"You just sit there and listen to me preach, and I won't pray for you at all." He said the largest percentage of that congregation was perfectly healed in just a little while. They came every day for 30 days. At the end of 30 days there was only about 7% of the whole congregation that was not healed. All they did was get healed spiritually. When you get healed spiritually, the chances are a hundred to one you will be healed physically.

Healing was the evidence of God's forgiveness — heaven's testimony that their sins were remembered no more.

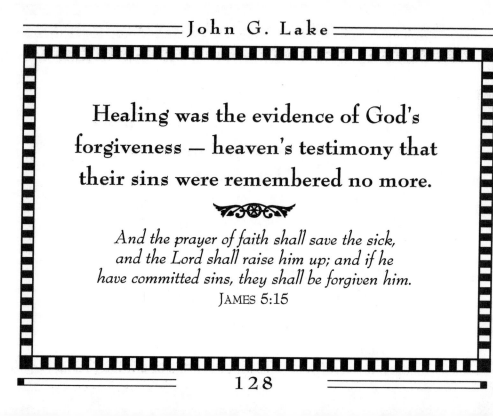

And the prayer of faith shall save the sick, and the Lord shall raise him up; and if he have committed sins, they shall be forgiven him.

JAMES 5:15

A God without power to heal
a sick heathen's body is a poor
recommendation of His ability
to save his soul.

*"But that you may know that the Son of Man has power
on earth to forgive sins" — then He said to the paralytic,
"Arise, take up your bed, and go to your house." And he
arose and departed to his house.*
MATTHEW 9:6,7 NKJV

God has made us as near like Himself as it is possible for God to make a being. He made you in His image. He made you in His likeness. He made you the same class of being that He is Himself.

What is man, that thou art mindful of him?
and the son of man, that thou visitest him?
For thou hast made him a little lower than the angels,
and hast crowned him with glory and honour.
PSALM 8:4,5

Jesus never intended Christians to be an imitation. They were to be bone of His bone, and blood of His blood, and flesh of His flesh, and soul of His soul, and spirit of His Spirit.

For we are members of his body, of his flesh, and of his bones.
EPHESIANS 5:30

Now if your faith is weak and sickly, it is because your spiritual connection with the Lord is faulty. Maybe there is a fuse blown. Maybe a switch is out. But there it is. Now there must be a right adjustment of the soul to the body and of soul and body and spirit.

And the very God of peace sanctify you wholly; and I pray God your whole spirit and soul and body be preserved blameless unto the coming of our Lord Jesus Christ.
1 Thessalonians 5:23

Real Christianity is marked by the pureness, the holiness of the thoughts of man; and if the kind of Christianity you have does not produce in your mind real holiness, real purity, real sweetness, real truth, then it is a poor brand. Change it right away.

To the pure all things are pure, but to those who are defiled and unbelieving nothing is pure; but even their mind and conscience are defiled.
TITUS 1:15 NKJV

If you are having the right kind
of spiritual fellowship, you will
have power with God, and there
is no escaping it.

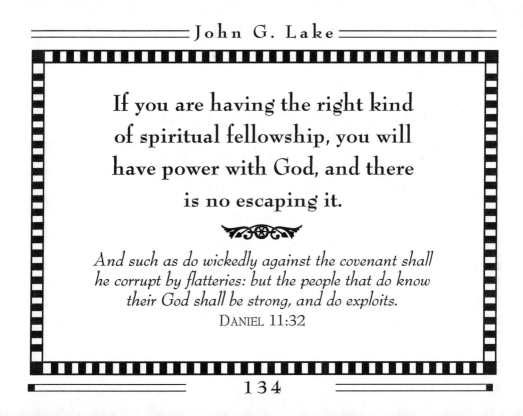

*And such as do wickedly against the covenant shall
he corrupt by flatteries: but the people that do know
their God shall be strong, and do exploits.*
DANIEL 11:32

Men have mystified the Gospel; they have philosophized the Gospel. The Gospel of Jesus is as simple as can be.

And my speech and my preaching was not with enticing words of man's wisdom, but in demonstration of the Spirit and of power.
1 CORINTHIANS 2:4

The preaching that lacks the signs which Jesus promised lacks Divine attestation, by which God confirms the preaching of His own true Gospel.

And they went forth, and preached every where, the Lord working with them, and confirming the word with signs following. Amen.
MARK 16:20

The Church is the generating power of God in the world; the Church has been negligent in one thing. She has not prayed the power of God out of heaven."

Who hath heard such a thing? who hath seen such things? Shall the earth be made to bring forth in one day? or shall a nation be born at once? for as soon as Zion travailed, she brought forth her children.

Isaiah 66:8

The sanest man is the man who believes God and stands on His promises, and knows the secret of His power, receives the Holy Ghost and gives Him sway in his life, and goes out in the Name of the Lord Jesus to command the will of God and bring it to pass in the world.

For God hath not given us the spirit of fear; but of power, and of love, and of a sound mind.
2 TIMOTHY 1:7

It is the conscious presence of the living, risen Son of God dwelling in our heart by the Holy Ghost, which causes you and I to know that the power of God is equal to every emergency and is great enough for the deliverance of every soul from every oppression.

But in all these things we overwhelmingly conquer through Him who loved us.
ROMANS 8:37 NAS

The Spirit of God emanating from Paul transformed the handkerchiefs into "storage batteries" of Holy Spirit power. When they were laid upon the sick they surcharged the body, and healing was the result.

This demonstrates, firstly: The Spirit of God is a tangible substance, heavenly materiality. Secondly: It is capable of being stored in the substance of a handkerchief, as demonstrated in the garments of Jesus, or in the handkerchiefs of Paul. Thirdly: It will transmit power from handkerchiefs to the sick person. Fourthly: Its action in the sick man was so powerful the disease departed. The demonized also were relieved. Fifthly: Both the sick and insane were healed by this method.

Here is the thing that is mightily important: that the spirit life in a man is kept healthy and vigorous — kept healthy and vigorous by three exercises. There are more ways, but three in particular: One is feeding on the Word. Second is a continual public confession of what you are and what Jesus is to you. I am not talking of sin. I mean confession of your faith in Christ, of what Christ is to you, of His fullness, of His completeness, and of His redemption. And the third thing is communion with Him. Feeding on the Word, confession, and communion. Three simple things, aren't they? And yet they are the things that produce great spiritual life. You do not have it without them.

A low standard of Christianity is responsible for much of the shame and sin and wickedness in the world.

You are the salt of the earth; but if the salt has become tasteless, how will it be made salty again? It is good for nothing anymore, except to be thrown out and trampled under foot by men.
MATTHEW 5:13 NAS

Christianity is not the product
of human reasoning. Christianity
is a divine intervention.

*How God anointed Jesus of Nazareth with the Holy Ghost
and with power: who went about doing good, and healing
all that were oppressed of the devil; for God was with him.*
ACTS 10:38

The devil's fears are always falsehoods. His suggestions are always lies, and if lies, they cannot harm. If fear comes from Satan, then we can conclude there is nothing to fear.

Be submissive then to God. Stand up to the devil and he will turn and run.
JAMES 4:7 NEB

There are so many preachers who are afraid of the devil. They have no idea of how big God is Who dwells in you. They have no idea of the power given to you because God dwells in you.

Behold, I give unto you power to tread on serpents and scorpions, and over all the power of the enemy: and nothing shall by any means hurt you.

LUKE 10:19

The aspiration of every teacher is to bring his student to his own level of understanding. The triumph of every teacher is to inspire within the student the possibility of even surpassing the teacher in his search for knowledge and truth.

And thou shalt teach them ordinances and laws, and shalt shew them the way wherein they must walk, and the work that they must do.
EXODUS 18:20

Everybody wants to jump in and preach, but bless God, when we are willing to go through with Jesus in that "getting ready" process, then it will be with effectiveness, it will be with power, it will be with the love of God.

The preparations of the heart in man, and the answer of the tongue, is from the LORD.
PROVERBS 16:1

A weak Christianity is ever inclined
to whine in prayer, while God waits
for the believer to command it.

*But lift thou up thy rod, and stretch out thine hand
over the sea, and divide it: and the children of Israel
shall go on dry ground through the midst of the sea.*
EXODUS 14:16

Real prayer is communion with God,
not just praying words, but getting
an answer from heaven.

*If ye abide in me, and my words abide in you, ye shall
ask what ye will, and it shall be done unto you.*

JOHN 15:7

But when your soul melts into that other life and your spirit melts into theirs, you will come to that place where Jesus was when He took upon Himself the sins of the world.

And of some have compassion, making a difference.
JUDE 1:22

No religion among the religions of the world has ever offered a solution for the sin problem. Jesus Christ alone has brought the solution.

But this man, after he had offered one sacrifice for sins for ever, sat down on the right hand of God.
HEBREWS 10:12

God's call to the Christian churches today
is to come forth from their hiding place,
just as Elijah came forth, and meet the King.
Declare the ground on which you meet
the enemies of God, and meet them
in the Name of Jesus Christ.

*"Answer me, O LORD, answer me, so these people will know that
you, O LORD, are God, and that you are turning their hearts back
again." Then the fire of the LORD fell and burned up the sacrifice,
the wood, the stones and the soil, and also licked up the water in the
trench. When all the people saw this, they fell prostrate and cried,
"The LORD – he is God! The LORD – he is God!"*
1 KINGS 18:37-39 NIV

The great majority of the Christian world is still weeping at the foot of the cross. The consciousness of man is fixed on the Christ Who died, not on the Christ Who lives. They are looking back to the Redeemer Who was, not the Redeemer Who is.

Seeing then that we have a great high priest, that is passed into the heavens, Jesus the Son of God, let us hold fast our profession.

HEBREWS 4:14

In my assembly at Spokane is a dear little woman who was totally blind for nine years. She had little teaching along the line of faith in God. She sat one day with her group of six children to discover that the dirty brute of a husband had abandoned her. A debased human being is capable of things that no beast will do, for a beast will care for its own. You can imagine what that little heart was like. She was broken and bruised and bleeding. She gathered her children around her and began to pray. They were sitting on their front porch.

Presently the little one got up and said, "Oh, Mama, there is a man coming up the path, and he looks like Jesus. Oh, Mama, there is blood on His hands and blood on His feet!" And the children were frightened and ran around the corner of the house. After a while the biggest one looked around the corner and said, "Why, Mama, He is laying His hands on your eyes!" And just then her blind eyes opened.

Man was never made a slave. He was never made for slavery. He was made to reign as king under God.

And have made us kings and priests to our God; and we shall reign on the earth.
REVELATION 5:10 NKJV

As long as your spirit is triumphant,
you are a victor and go right on.
A man is defeated only when he
is defeated in his spirit.

The human spirit will endure sickness;
but a broken spirit — who can bear?
PROVERBS 18:14 NRSV

Bible References

Additional copies of this book available from your local bookstore.
⛉ HARRISON HOUSE · Tulsa, Oklahoma 74153

In Canada books are available from: Word Alive
P. O. Box 670 · Niverville, Manitoba · CANADA R0A 1E0

The Harrison House Vision

Proclaiming the truth and the power
Of the Gospel of Jesus Christ
With excellence;

Challenging Christians to
Live victoriously,
Grow spiritually,
Know God intimately.